THE SORROW STONE

A COLLECTION OF POETRY ABOUT GRIEF, LOSS, AND HOPE

BY

D. D. ROEBKE

© 2013 by David D. Roebke

Electronic Edition publisher:
Bookbaby, Portland, OR

Printed Edition publisher:
Create Space 4900 La Crosse Road
North Charleston, SC 29406
USA

ISBN 13-978-0615810256
ISBN 10-061581025X
 .

Printed first in the United States

Electronic Edition first published April 24, 2013

Print Edition first published June 2013

Cover Art: Concept David Roebke, Art: Bookbaby

Distributed by Create Space, a division of Amazon Inc.

FOR JEAN

Foreword

On April 7, 2010, I lost my best friend and confidant, to a rare cancer after an eight-month struggle. She was a superb woman with a quick sense of humor who loved God.

Jean was worth every courtesy; every drop of sweat, cold night, hot day and long separation. It was so easy to love her that I describe our relationship as a "dance."

This poetry was my approach to the journey through loss to healing. To my surprise, this poetry is currently being used in psychiatric therapy to help others, as I hoped.

Perhaps you may wish to write about your challenge? I've provided several blank pages at the end where you may add your thoughts. I make no promises, only share my poetry and hope you see in me a fellow traveler on the trail to recovery. Please scan the QR codes and listen to me read. I will always miss her.

Author: D. D. Roebke "The Sorrow Stone,"
© 2013. Comments: thesorrowstone@new.rr.com

Remembrance

They tap me on the shoulder,
And speak to me in distant tones,
They call at night, when dark is light,
And ask for my attention,
I entertain them, sometimes,
And they entertain me,
Appearing, then gone to recall,
Their own memories,
To stalk deserted halls and,
Walk where figures remain,
In storage,
Then take their places, waiting
For me to remember them again,
And they, to remember me.

Contents

It's Empty Here

I wait for her in empty halls,
In night-calls, deep in half-there sleep,
A dream-walked twilight, running in place,
No end for the endless timed-out race,

I see the one where two once owned,
I see the trail with footsteps on,
Looking at the stepping stones flat stare,
A quick punishing look now reflects,

Empty shoes, empty steps in, out,
Where once tones of higher order fell,
A still reigns where mind-steps tell,
A plot, a stand, a stone without hands,

No going, no coming, no greeting to come,
It's six feet of silence finally done.

This Way

How loud is the silence surrounding this way,
To stand stock and bare as in sun's searing day,
No mirrors are found, no reflection of light,
'Falling, fainting away,' the grief-chanteys' say,

It creeps by inches and leaps by bounds,
It yells and is silent with uncertain sounds,
No leader, no guide for this sorrow's lone trail,
No pause at the silence, but move to the ground,

Where are you peace, where are you joy,
Where is remittance these things employ?
How wide is the way, how wide is the walk,
To find sorrow's ending, an end to it sought,

Loss, a fog, a mist covering harm,
But with loss comes what I would not invite,
The way of ends, the way not warm,
Nor wish on another sorrow's lonely fight.

Sorrow Tree

It hangs like fruit on a heavy tree,
Branches borne down, to a somber ground,
They fall every-then but never to seed,
When done, hardly noise from solid sound,

It follows like a lost puppy nipping at my heals,
A bother, I pick up and pet, then put back down,
Now loud, barking with eyes memory feels,
Lost but found in a forlorn now?

Pushed away like a bad meal, unwanted,
Vaunted as a door never dodged, needed,
The fruit falls, one by one, not desired,
And lost 'when bough breaks', gone when picked,

A visitor unwelcome, brings joy when spent,
Hurried but stubborn like a wart, stark, bare,
A blemish forcing grief to bloom in time,
Like the fall of each fruit, like tasting lime,

The end of love-life, a blanket thrown off,
A bane, a hound baying at the sun,
Piercing sounds, deafening, a desire lost,
A lamenting sob, a lost lost, solemn, sings alone.

Look Back

They call to me in silent tomes,
When night is near the door,
No steps to place on entry's way,
No voice to call out, "Come away,"

It falls as leaden snow descends,
Where dark defines the edges ends,
And sight will follow border's call,
Advance, retreat through door, in hall,

It sheds its dark where light once danced,
And shadow where the bold once chanced,
"Come away," it calls in a twilight pall,
To walk a walk where memories fall,

I see in there shards of true light,
Not all is dim, as truth declares,
No struggle there, no call to fight,
Just pieces of where love once dared.

An Exercise in Ends

No day is day without a night,
No wrong is wrong without a right,
No blind is blind without true sight,

No in is in without an out,
No call out-loud without a shout,
No death a death without a life,

Throw up a thing, it must come down,
Look at the sky, it's from the ground,
Add two plus two, it must be four,

Start a book, it has an end,
To receive a thing, it must be sent,
Take off a shoe, it must be on,
Listen to silence, there must be sound,
To roll a ball, it must be round,

In order to listen, One must hear,
Make a sound, talk in a rhyme,
Take a watch, speak the time,
Make some sound, make a voice,
Take a number, make a choice,
Final is final to the world,
That's not in God's economy.

My Loss

Holding breath, I look for life,
No life is found in moving time,
The day flies by, breath still in,
A gasping, clawing, to prove a win,

The game is past, my helmet down,
My shoes on side, sword on the ground,
I stand and kneel before truth's One,
My breath still here, no letting out,

Oh, fill my thoughts with pleasant days,
When love's breath breathed in normal ways,
When this heart moved and danced on wings,
Now feather bare, now rocks and things,

Oh let love's seed see life once more,
In fallow ground, in soil so poor,
A rift twixt two let seed so fall,
To bring breath new and heart to soar.
©2012 D. D. Roebke

Through The Wall

Push and push through the wall,
A barrier of time has grown so tall,
Hard to see victory inside the small,
No hand to lay, no physical display,

That 'small deadly space' where sorrow treads,
A dangerous place for truths unsaid,
A narrow path where others go,
No desire to pursue nor move ahead,

Footsteps fall on paths rarely tread,
My footfalls follow in surreal pace,
To move one, power flees the time,
One step advanced, one stays in place,

Crawling is a true-grown state,
Hands and knees up to the wall,
Push forward using my head,
But bruises find my downcast pate,

Futility beckons from the sides,
"No victory there, rest o'er here,"
It quotes no hope, no white horse rides,
I learn to stand ... no "Spirit of fear."

Her Ways

I look for her in special days,
In garden's flowers in her ways,
Walking talking following the Lord,
Pursuing, doing, and serving God,

When clouds pass on, she's in my lens,
She's in the trees and 'remember whens',
Her face before me night and day,
Her touch and laugh now only then,

Thoughts move through a cavalcade,
Of ways and decisions we together made,
No peace-found days in this past charade,
Posing as a day's parade but past,

No comfort in this indie film of life,
Showing snatches of her and gone,
Senses can't send a sign of now,
Mere shadow of the then and done.

This Life's Scene

To laugh and dance is rarely seen,
In this life's show, not puzzling,
The time, the clock, the piece had been,
The wolf's prey chasing twilight's scene,

I matched her step, she held my arm,
I held her chair, I opened her door,
She touched my face, that paid it all,
But life's beyond that faded charm,

My love lives like a memory,
That sometimes goes and comes to me,
An 'ever steady mark' this storm still on,
To toss love's wave and travel free,

A longing there in rarefied air,
Gasping for some purchase place,
To laugh and dance is rarely seen,
In this life's show, not puzzling.

Flat Love

My future flat, in dust, in iron,
That two-part harmony is done,
The future's dust can't be un-urned,
The future died, the future burned,

Such sober sense and tears shed then,
But thoughts must go and time must bow,
Life moves forward in part-time now,
A fleeting thought, a maybe when,

Grief's whip falls much in sorrow's den,
Where broken heart comes to visit and,
Crawls back to stage and plays the fool,
A jeering mind, no empathetic end,

Two dimensions prod at me,
Heart hides often out of habit,
Its ache a world's psychology,
Who knows its ways? Who knows it sees?

Lord I pray grief takes a trip,
Far away, lets go its grip,
Let heart arise, let heart go free,
Oh Holy One be balm to me.

Life after Death

That day floats before my face,
Like a lost balloon, with no hiding place,
Single footsteps run the life-K,
Now for heaven's door there is no race,

The smell, the bags, the constant care,
Pull at thoughts when grief will dare,
No peace in the following, though peace is won,
A two-edged sword now cuts one way,

Birds and trees bring thought to mind,
Of gentle hands, a view so kind,
The will is wrote, the will is done,
No comfort in these things will find,

Running by day, walking by night,
Living by touch, a blinded man's sight,
'Making much of time' a burden of right,
Gentle hands flee, and gardens go bare,
A poor man's place, a straggler's share.

Listening for Love's Pale Light

Love's pale shine leaves no soul-rest,
It prods at night, a foot-stepped test,
No fun to see it fall 'round my heart,
Love's pale shine shows this harmony flat,

A need, a want, pale light shows who,
Expressed here and there with single eye,
No 'love's pale light' keeps dark at bay,
But spirit may say, "Leave it that way,"

A desire burned there, a 'should' burned here,
No sure place found but hints at fear,
"Dust to dust" life's forlorn call,
No comfort left, no steadfast dear,

Come hear my now, come hear me say,
A life of love following in God's way,
That life goes on out of my sight,
But memories on and on will play,
Pale light come another day.

My Beloved's Voice

Calming was my beloved's voice,
A smooth un-taxing sound to hear,
Her tones a welcome thing through then,
Now sounds of past repetition there,

Looked forward to by night, by day,
Laughter, true life's following sight,
Love saying, "Yes" and dwelling here,
A verbal dance of love's spoken tears,

Echoes roam both inside-out,
Both loud and soft, whisper, shout,
All parts of one, unique to find,
That love's true voice in memory's ear,

Where is that soul, where is that one,
Where is the voice I cherish on?
A spoken sob, a groaned despair,
Desiring life to that voice again.

Love Laugh

Love beckons me like a jester's wand,
To look beyond the time's dark days,
And find again love's lost beyonds,
To share love's laugh so plainly gone,

I stare with catatonic gaze,
At love's lost art, no frames, displays,
A proper joy love's mindless ways,
And sit in juxtaposed mirror's face,

Love laugh for me so I know the tones,
Not hear past grief's bereft alones,
Find place again in love's fine land,
Solid hearts in love's second-hand.

Writer's Block

Silently the sole sonnet writer sits,
His pen a reprimand of story-told wit,
No sonnet there, no limerick found,
Just pen and sheet with a solitary sound,

A stare in time, daydream's brief realm.

A reach toward memories vault ensues,
But blocks and walls forbid the reach,
For thought of good and fair, pen pursues,
And sheets lay bare, no virtue greets,

Where is the tale of light's true sight?
The story of grief's ultimate end?
It lay in gold Spirit-seen streets,
And balks at 'Zebra Storyteller's' intent.

No. Love ends here, though pens do rage,
And hands use power to write them on,
A lines-traded bar, a two-stepped page,
Where goodness flees from dark's bright sun,
But goodness tells of life fairly won.

What If?

If I had done what I had thought,
The "if" would find what doubt had wrought,
If's wandering ways tries finding a life,
In emotions discarded, time unsought,

It chases doubters down a lonely trail,
To regret's lost fen, to epic fail,
Time's friend in mind leaves faces pale,
It steps on heartstring's fragile pace,

An accuser's whip, it strikes when one,
Prodding self with doubt's sharp dig,
And tying down soul in noonday sun,
Then eaten by self's army ants to find,
Bones of grief when found alone.

Ultimate day

Five fingers, a door, a chair, a car,
Love's mournful stare, five fingers bare,
A vessel, a vase to pour love in,
Love knows an end when favors fade,

Windless, unyielding, fateful, fall,
It hides and will only show when hunted,
No fear when seen, it sits and sits,
The vessel loses its lustered view,

One breath, one tone, a forlorn sigh,
Love lasts, exhaustion there, no will,
Love spills as the vessel breaks in bits,
The dust of ending in the iron it fits.

Longing's Long Trail

The soldier says stand, though heart not in,
A Roman unseen by eyes not there,
That hazel view adored so clearly then,
No justice for the soldier's ends,

A long, long walk, four feet on two,
A cadence there not shared by fate,
No fate to find but God's clear way,
A soldier's "goodbye," a stone's forever stare,

Where is the love I knew from far,
Then saw so close, it found my heart,
And stayed so solid in sure rich soil,
Facing storms, gale, and high seas roil?

The catamaran, now single hulled,
The taxed a voice no longer two,
A place so large life's laughter fades,
Echoes of a long lost days' parades.

She Dances

She dances through my dimming eyes,
A faded fancy fairly found,
But lost in fog of daily reprise,
Now found in places most despised,

A length of love measured there,
Time-traveled footfalls singly done,
Her look, her smell, a daytime stare,
A touch, a kiss, a skin-sensed sun,

A step and step one now, one then,
A dance, a fugue, a pauper's ken,
She dances, phantoms only now.

Time's Long Stride

Walking slowly, stepping by hour,
Finding, losing the next step away,
Standing crawling, then looking for power,
Never arriving but praying for the day,

Looking hard, not seeing, but knowing,
Expecting no solace for sight sought,
Squinting, trying to see the unseen,
A dimension of two, all desire is flat,

Reaching not touching, the air is dry,
Stretching backward to touch lost time,
Pointing, extending, my arm's lost, sigh,
A longing, the skin at rest, locked in rhyme,

A longer step, there footfalls stand,
In places never known, an idiot's shuffle,
The dark is found but not a friend,
The ultimate step, the day's not enough.

Sorrow Stones

It's there, I carry it around,
Like a pile of stones in one hand,
Constantly dropping and picking up,
More one day, less on another,

I try to juggle them, they fall,
I leave them behind, they call,
I throw them away, they come back,
How strange I look carrying these stones.

One day, Lord, help me put them down,
Let them fall, let them stay,
Help me carry them by night,
Lay them down in the day.

Lord these stones are heavy,
My legs are sore, my back is bowed,
It's been so long, so long since then,
Help me hold them and let them go.

Grief Locusts

Night came on silent wings,
It brought the dark and other things,
They didn't go "bump," or make a sound,
No feeling by touch, but they stayed around,

They followed like locusts, breaking in,
No bites I could see, no wounds in sight,
But gnawing, eating and stealing breath,
A wound forming unseen but seen,

Breathing in, out, regular, not,
Slowly, slowly, Finding no rest,
One hour here, two hours there,
One day here, two days there,

A box, four corners inside out,
Dark inside, other things abide,
No place to hide from it,
No way to wrest away from it,
No will to stay away from it.

Who Am I?

Who am I, really am I?
A part of me is gone,
No more to show that face,
No more to keep that place,

He's sad, he's alone, he's there,
Eyes looking on in tears,
And derision, for no decision,
Lay there for me to find,

Where is the man, the male?
He stands in rain and hail,
And can't come in, not in,
I just stand there in the rain and hail.

He's there-in the night,
He's near but far, he has no sight,
He's looking down, yes down,
No comfort there, but rain,
No feeling there, so hail.

Lonely but Not Alone

The longest day is a lonely night,
The Spirit's way leads to the right,
A loss, a trial not longer in sight,
The Loneliest day is the longest night,

Forever is a way to see,
How love will last eternally,
Please help this blind one finally see,
What You have, what is for me,

A corner turned is a corner gone,
What's found is found, heart goes on,
Heart will find where true love points,
And give new life where love anoints,

No rest is there, no rest is found,
In lonely days when heart is bound,
Love loose the chains of night in here,
Lord hear my plea, bring mercy near.

NOTES

NOTES

NOTES

NOTES

END

www.ingramcontent.com/pod-product-compliance
Lightning Source LLC
Chambersburg PA
CBHW060551030426
42337CB00019B/3516